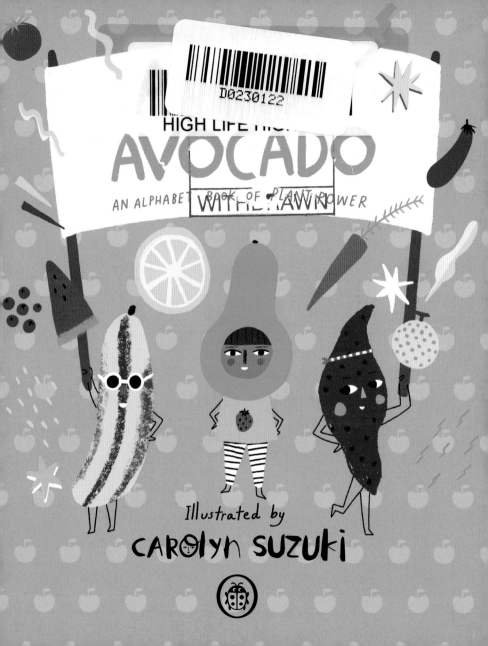

HIGH LIFE HIGH

AVOCADO

AN ALPHABET BOOK OF PLANT POWER

WITHDRAWN

Illustrated by

CAROLYN SUZUKI

A

AVOCADO

The Aztecs used these rich, creamy fruits as a symbol of love

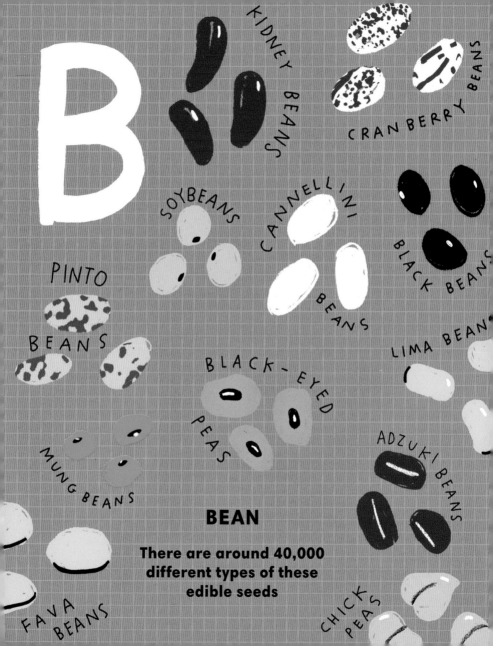

B

KIDNEY BEANS

CRANBERRY BEANS

SOYBEANS

CANNELLINI BEANS

BLACK BEANS

PINTO BEANS

BLACK-EYED PEAS

LIMA BEAN

ADZUKI BEANS

MUNG BEANS

BEAN

There are around 40,000 different types of these edible seeds

FAVA BEANS

CHICK PEAS

CARROT

Carrots contain beta-carotene, a chemical that can improve your eyesight

DURIAN

This strong-smelling fruit is highly prized throughout South East Asia

E

ELDERBERRY

These tart berries grow in clusters and are harvested in the autumn

ELDE

FENNEL

The flowers, leaves, seeds and bulb of the fennel plant are all edible

GRAPE

Grapes are berries that grow in a variety of colours, from green to black

HONEYDEW MELON

In ancient Egypt, only the wealthy were allowed to eat this sweet melon

I

ICEBERG LETTUCE

This lettuce used to be transported on ice to keep it fresh, which is how it got its name

J

JACKFRUIT

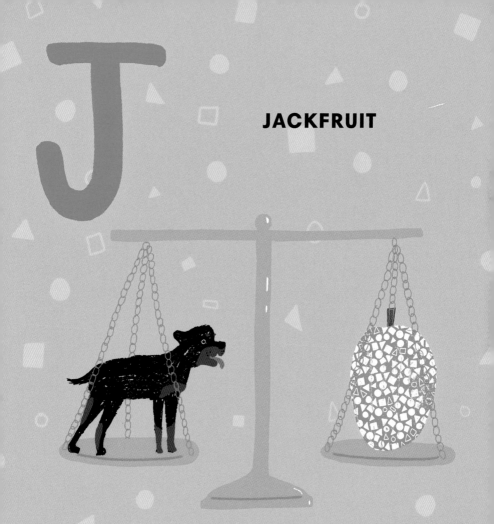

**Jackfruits can weigh up to forty-five kilograms –
the same as a Rottweiler dog**

KALE

One handful of this leafy vegetable has more vitamin C than an entire orange

LENTIL

These protein-packed circular seeds grow together in tiny pods

M

MUSHROOM

**More than sixty species
of mushroom can glow
in the dark**

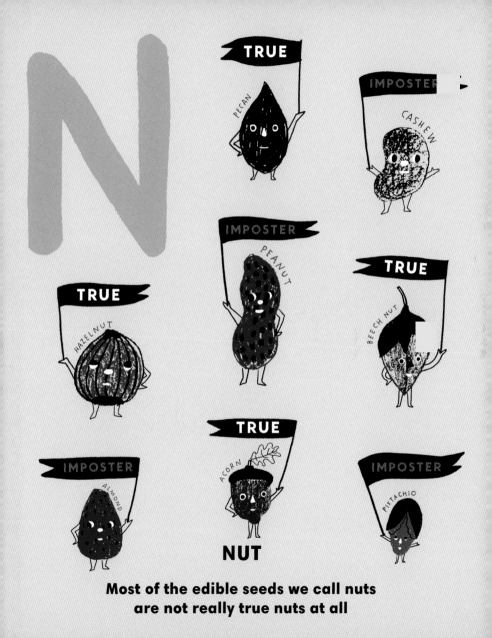

Most of the edible seeds we call nuts are not really true nuts at all

ONION

Onions contain acids that are safe to eat,
but can make you cry when you cut into them

PLANTAIN

These 'cooking bananas' are often served fried, mashed or boiled

Q

QUINCE

Quince paste, or cheese, is a jelly made from this hard pear-shaped fruit

RADISH

This fast-growing plant takes just four weeks to grow from a seed

SWEET POTATO

Sweet potatoes are in a separate plant
family from other varieties of potato

T

TOFU

Blocks of soybean curd have been used as a meat substitute for over 2,000 years

UGLI FRUIT

This Jamaican citrus fruit is part grapefruit and part orange

VEGETARIAN AND VEGAN

Vegetarians and vegans eat plant-based diets

TAHINI

BEANS

ALMOND MILK

WATERMELON

Ninety-two per cent of a watermelon
is water, which explains its name!

XIMENIA FRUIT

This African sour plum is a popular snack for both birds and humans

Y

YAM

This starchy root vegetable is related to the lily flower

Z

ZUCCHINI

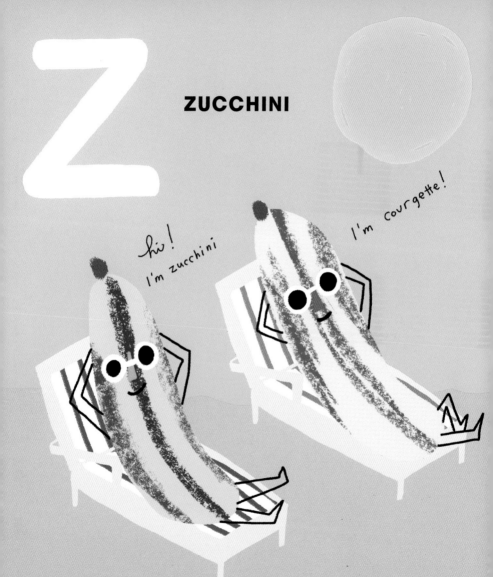

This summer squash is also called a courgette